FOLLOWING JESUS

From the Moving Toward Maturity Series

Barry St. Clair

Moving Toward Maturity Series
> *Getting Started*
> *Following Jesus* (Book 1)
> *Spending Time Alone with God* (Book 2)
> *Making Jesus Lord* (Book 3)
> *Giving Away Your Faith* (Book 4)
> *Influencing Your World* (Book 5)
> *Moving Toward Maturity Series Leader's Guide*
> *Spending Time Alone with God Notebook*

Produced by REACH OUT YOUTH SOLUTIONS
> 3961 Holcomb Bridge Road
> Suite 201
> Norcross, GA 30092

ISBN: 1-931617-07-4

1 2 3 4 5 6 7 8 9 10 Printing/Year 10 09 08 07 06 05 04 03 02 01

The usage of the pronouns "his/he/him" has been used throughout this book for the sake of continuity and uniformity. The reader should assume these references refer to both male and female.

GREAT STUFF IN THE BOOK

SPECIAL THANKS

To Rod Minor and Debbie Hayes for originally working on this project with me.

To Burt Stouffer and Ernest Pullen for designing and packaging the *Moving Toward Maturity* Series.

To the youth ministers from across the country who have tested this material and given valuable suggestions.

To my late wife Carol and my children Scott and Cameron, Katie and Bart, Jonathan, and Ginny, who have loved me and encouraged me in my ministry.

To Lawanna, my wife, my fellow struggler in death and life, and my heart's companion for the second half of my life.

To the Lord Jesus Christ for teaching me the realities in this book.

A WORD FROM THE AUTHOR

Jesus Christ has made positive changes in my life. He can change your life too. And He can use you to change others!

Just make yourself AVAILABLE and Jesus can:

 ⟶ Help you to know Him better.

 ⟶ Work in you to make you a more mature Christian.

 ⟶ Motivate you to share Christ with others.

 ⟶ Use you to help others grow toward maturity.

 ⟶ Lead you to lead others.

My goal for you: "Just as you received Christ Jesus as Lord, continue to live in Him, rooted and built up in Him, strengthened in the faith as you were taught, and overflowing with thankfulness" (Colossians 2:6-7).

When that is happening in your life, then just as 2 x 2 = 4, and 4 x 4 = 16, and on to infinity, so Jesus can use you to multiply His life in others to make an impact on the world. How? One Christian (like you) leads another person to Christ and helps him/her move toward maturity.

Then the new believer leads another person to Christ and helps him/her move toward maturity. And so the process continues. God gives you the tremendous privilege of knowing Him and making Him known to others. That is what your life and the *Moving Toward Maturity* series are all about.

The *Moving Toward Maturity* series includes a book for new believers entitled *Getting Started* and five discipleship books designed to help you grow in Christ and become a significant part of the multiplication process. *Following Jesus* is the first book in the series. The other books are:

Spending Time Alone with God (Book 2)
Making Jesus Lord (Book 3)
Giving Away Your Faith (Book 4)
Influencing Your World (Book 5)

God's desire and my prayer for you is that the things you discover on the following pages will become not just a part of your notes, but a part of your life. May all that's accomplished in your life be to His honor and glory.

Barry

PURPOSE

This book will help you grasp the basics of living life with Jesus Christ and will get you started on the path of true discipleship.

Discipleship can be partially defined as:

➡️> becoming independently dependent on Jesus Christ and

➡️> teaching people to be taught by God.

Paul summarized the personal discipleship process when he said, "(I am) confident of this, that He who began a good work in you will carry it on to completion until the day of Christ Jesus" (Philippians 1:6).

Before you begin doing the Bible studies in this book, make the commitment to let Jesus Christ bring to completion all He wants to do in your life.

USES FOR
THIS BOOK

1. SMALL GROUPS: You can use this book as a member of an organized group (Discipleship Group) led by an adult leader.* Each person in this group signs the commitment sheet on page 11, and agrees to use the book week by week for personal growth.

2. INDIVIDUALS: You can go through this book on your own, doing one lesson each week for your own personal growth.

3. NON-BELIEVING FRIENDS: You can ask a friend who has expressed an interest in Jesus Christ but who is not yet a believer to join you in a weekly time of studying and sharing together with the hope that he/she will follow Jesus.

4. DISCIPLING YOUNGER STUDENTS: After you apply each session in this book to your own life, you can help a younger person or younger group work through *Following Jesus*.

---

*The Leader's Guide for the *Moving Toward Maturity* series can be purchased from Reach Out Youth Solutions. See the order information in the back of this book.

PRACTICAL HINTS

(How to get the most out of this book)

If you want to grow as a Christian, you must get real with God and apply the Bible to your life. Sometimes that's hard, but this book can help you if you will:

1. Begin each session with prayer.
    Ask God to speak to you.

2. Use a Bible that's easy to read.
    Try the *New International Version*.

3. Work through the entire session.
    ⁃⟩ Look up the Bible verses.
    ⁃⟩ Think through the answers.
    ⁃⟩ Write the answers.
    ⁃⟩ Jot down any questions you have.
    ⁃⟩ Memorize the assigned verse(s).
        (Use the Bible memory cards in the back of the book. Groups should select a single translation to memorize, in order to recite the verse(s) together.)

4. Apply each session to your life.
    ⁃⟩ Ask God to show you how to act on what you're learning from His Word.
    ⁃⟩ Obey Him in your relationships, attitudes, and actions.
    ⁃⟩ Talk over the results with other believers who can encourage and advise you.

IF YOU'RE IN A DISCIPLESHIP GROUP

➤ Set aside two separate times each week to work on the assigned Session. If possible, complete the whole Bible Study during the first time. Then during the second time (the day of or the day before your next group meeting), review what you've learned.

➤ Take your Bible, this book, and a pen or pencil to every group meeting.

PERSONAL
COMMITMENT

I, _____, hereby
dedicate myself to the following commitments:

1. To submit myself daily to God and to all that He wants to teach me about growing as a follower of Jesus.

2. To attend all weekly group meetings unless a serious illness or circumstance makes that impossible. If I miss more than one meeting, I will withdraw willingly from the group if it is determined necessary after meeting with the group leader.

3. To complete the assignments without fail as they are due each week.

4. To be actively involved in my local church.

I understand that these commitments are not only to the Lord but to the group and to myself as well. With God's help, I will do my very best to completely fulfill each one.

Signed_____ Date _____

Answering important questions

When you walk into class on Monday morning and discover you blew it on Friday's test, what difference does it make if you have a personal relationship with Jesus Christ?

A person without Jesus Christ has no resources outside of himself to deal with the problems that smack him in the face every day. But, a follower of Jesus can handle any problem or frustration by focusing on the resources available through Jesus Christ.

You'll discover what some of those resources are throughout the ten Bible studies in this book. But to tap into them for your own life, you must be able to answer three basic questions in your mind and heart:

-> What is a Christian?

-> How do you become a Christian?

-> How do you know if you're really a Christian?

WHAT IS A CHRISTIAN?
Why do you think God created you?

_____

_____

_____

Read 1 John 1:3 to discover God's perspective on why He created you. Now, how would you answer that question?

_____

_____

_____

A Christian is someone who has a personal relationship with Jesus Christ. But that relationship is not something you're born with, earn, or buy.

Look at Romans 3:23 and 6:23.

-> SIN means to "miss the mark." It means going your way instead of God's way and, therefore, being separated from God.

-> DEATH means "spiritual separation."

To solve the problems of sin and death and to bring us into a personal relationship with Himself, God did something unique and amazing. Read Romans 5:8; 1 Corinthians 15:3-4; 1 Peter 3:18.

Write in your own words what God did.

_____

_____

_____

_____

Now check the following verses from the Gospel of John to see why Jesus came:

1:4 _____

1:11-13 _____

1:17 _____

2:19-22 _____

3:3 _____

3:16 _____

 Read Philippians 2:6-11. Though He didn't have to, Jesus willingly gave up the privileges of heaven with God his Father, and came to earth in human form to experience life as you experience it. Think about that for a minute.

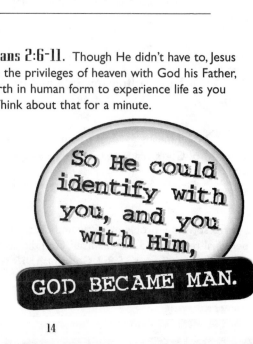

So He could identify with you, and you with Him,

GOD BECAME MAN.

Jesus faced the same kinds of struggles you face:
• disappointment
• rejection
• hurt
• sadness
• anger
• physical pain
• broken relationships

But He also gave His very life for you. Because He loved you so much, He willingly endured the humiliation and pain of death on the cross to pay the penalty for your sin.

As you think about what Jesus Christ did for you, what emotions do you feel?

_____

_____

HOW DO YOU BECOME A CHRISTIAN?

How do you think a person becomes a Christian? Write your opinion below.

_____

_____

_____

_____

_____

_____

_____

Does what you've written agree with God's thoughts? To make sure, look at the following five steps to become a Christian.

5 STEPS TO RECEIVE CHRIST:

At each step, read the Scripture passages and answer the questions. Then read the additional comments and, in the space provided, write how you have already responded or need to respond to each step.

Admit You Need Jesus

According to Romans 3:10, why do you need Jesus?

_____

_____

_____

_____

Basic human nature is rebellious and opposes God. It can cause you to say, "I don't need God."

GRACE IS:

"the free gift of God" given to help you turn to Jesus and to supply you with the power to live for Him.

But because of God's grace you can say, "I need God." God offers grace to you so you can admit that you need Him.

How does Step 1 relate to you?

_____

_____

_____

_____

_____

2 **Turn from Your Sins**

What does Mark 1:15 say to you about turning from your sins?

_____

_____

_____

REPENT MEANS:

"to turn around"-- to turn away from a self-centered, self-controlled life.

How does Step 2 relate to you?

_____

_____

_____

_____

_____

(3) Give Your Life to Christ

From John 1:12 and 2 Corinthians 5:15, what do you need to do to give your life to Christ?

_____

_____

_____

_____

_____

CHRISTIAN MEANS:

"Christ in one."
Christ lives in you.
He comes to take
control of
your life.

How does Step 3 relate to you?

_____

_____

_____

_____

_____

_____

(4) **Believe That Jesus Lives in You and Gives You Eternal Life**

What does John 3:16-18 say about believing in Christ?

_____

_____

_____

How does Step 4 relate to you?

_____

_____

_____

_____

BELIEVE MEANS:

"total trust" – trusting Jesus now and every day.

_____

_____

_____

5

Follow Christ in Obedience

From John 8:31 and Romans 10:8-10, what are your first steps of obedience?

_____

_____

_____

_____

Baptism is an initial way to identify with Christ's death, burial, and resurrection. What are some other ways you can continue to identify with Him? Look up Matthew 28:18-20, Acts 2:41-47, and Acts 8:35-39. Then write your answer.

_____

_____

_____

_____

_____

_____

OBEDIENCE MEANS:

saying yes to Jesus about every decision, every day.

__I__II

How does Step 5 relate to you?

_____

_____

_____

_____

These steps to becoming a Christian can lead you to a personal relationship with Jesus Christ. Go back and look at the five steps asking yourself, "Where am I in my personal relationship to Jesus?"

1.
_____

_____

2.
_____

_____

3.
_____

_____

4.
_____

_____

5.
_____

_____

HOW DO YOU KNOW IF YOU'RE REALLY A CHRISTIAN?

Open your Bible to one of the most exciting books in the New Testament—I John. It contains so much about what Jesus Christ has done for you. Check it out.

According to 1 John 5:11-13, what can you know?

_____

_____

_____

_____

Read 1 John 2:3-5:1. How can you know if you're truly a Christian – a child of God? Write down what you learn from each set of verses.

2:3-6

_____

_____

_____

3:14

_____

_____

_____

3:24; 4:13

_____

_____

_____

4:15

_____

_____

_____

5:1

_____

_____

_____

MAKING IT PERSONAL

If you haven't asked Jesus into your life, you can do so right now. This prayer will guide you:

> "Lord Jesus, I admit that I am selfish. I confess my sins, turn from them, and ask You to come into my life. I give my life to You, Jesus. I ask You to take control of every area. More than anything else in the world, I want to follow and obey You. Amen."

If you have already asked Jesus into your life, thank Him for living in you. As you pray, tell Him the reason you know for sure that He lives in you, and that you have a personal relationship to Him.

 Memorize 1 John 5:11.

THE GREAT DISCOVERY

Discovering God's purpose for your life

Finish this sentence:

My purpose in life is

_____

_____

_____

_____

Does the purpose you've written here match God's purpose for your life? Let's check it out.

GOD'S 1st PURPOSE
God Wants A Love Relationship With You
In your own words, what does Matthew 22:36-38 say about your purpose in life?

_____

_____

_____

Your relationship starts with new birth. You become God's child.

Your relationship with God leads to fellowship –a process of daily living in harmony with God as your Father. Your Father loves you. He always will, no matter what. Your earthly father may or may not love you, but God your Father loves you completely! If you rebel against your Heavenly Father and do what you know is wrong (sin), your relationship with God is not severed, but your fellowship with Him is damaged.

How can you restore your fellowship with God and stay in harmony with Him?

Restore Fellowship
What do you do when sin in your life has caused your fellowship with God to be broken? To answer that question, read I John 1:9, underline it in your Bible, and circle the word "confess."

CONFESSION RESTORES FELLOWSHIP. But what does confession mean? Take a closer look.

To confess sin means two things:

➤ To agree with God that what you did is sin and that it is wrong.

➤ To stop doing what you did.

Spend some time alone in prayer right now. Ask God to bring to mind any unconfessed sins in your life. Write them on a separate piece of paper.

Then, on the promise of I John 1:9, CONFESS those sins by name, and thank God for His forgiveness and cleansing. As a symbol of your belief that God has done as He promised, burn the list.

Remain in Fellowship

Spending time communicating with another person keeps your relationship alive and helps your love for that person grow.

This is clearly evident in a dating relationship or close friendship. It also holds true in your fellowship with Christ. The more time you spend with Him—getting to know Him—the deeper your relationship grows.

COMMUNICATION DEEPENS YOUR RELATIONSHIP WITH JESUS. But how can you communicate with God?

Read Hebrews 4:12,16 and complete the statements.

➡ Listening to God through _____

➡ Talking to God through _____

My 1st purpose in life is: _____

_____

GOD'S 2nd PURPOSE

God wants you to move toward maturity in Christ

In your own words, what does Romans 8:29 say about your purpose in life?

_____

_____

_____

_____

Why is growing to become more and more like Jesus an important purpose?

➨〉 You will please God (Matthew 3:17).

➨〉 You will have a growing sense of fulfillment and joy (John 15:11).

Success is fulfilling your purpose in life. Just as a pen is successful when it writes, you're successful when you fulfill the purpose God has designed for you—being like Jesus.

If that's one of your purposes, then pursue that purpose with passion!

How can you pursue that purpose?

➨〉 By allowing Jesus' Spirit (Christ in you) and His Word to remold your words, thoughts, attitudes, and actions from the inside out (Galatians 5:19-23; Romans 12:2).

From these verses describe how that can happen to you.

_____

_____

➨〉 By letting God use everything that happens to you make you more like Jesus (Romans 8:28-29).

From these verses describe how that can happen to you.

_____

_____

My 2nd purpose in life is:_____

_____

GOD'S 3rd PURPOSE
God wants you to help others find new life in Christ

What does Mark 1:17 say about this purpose for your life?

_____

_____

_____

_____

_____

_____

How can you help others find new life in Christ?

➙〉 By showing Jesus to others through your changed attitudes and actions (Matthew 5:14-16). After reading these verses, think of ways He's changing you and write them here:

_____

_____

_____

➙〉 By telling others how Jesus has changed you and how they can know Him too (2 Corinthians 5:16-20).

In referring to the "Law of the Harvest," the Apostle Paul said that a person reaps in proportion to what he sows (2 Corinthians 9:6-11). Faith operates on this same principle. One of the best ways to increase your faith in Jesus Christ is to share Him with others! The more you give Him away, the more your faith will grow!

GOD'S PURPOSE:

Love Him.
Mature in Him.
Help others
find Him.

MAKING IT PERSONAL

Take 20 minutes

to look over this session and think about all of the insights you've gained. Then write your purpose in life as you now see it.

_____

_____

_____

_____

_____

_____

_____

_____

 Memorize Philippians 1:6.

S E S S I O N   3

Receiving God's love

Think about love as you've experienced it so far in your life.

In this heart, write words that describe your positive experiences with love.

In this heart, write words that describe your negative experiences with love.

"Love comes from God" (I John 4:7). It originates with Him. He is the source of love. Yet some people have a hard time accepting God's love. Why? Because their understandings of love are either inadequate or warped by negative experiences with human love. To get an accurate view of true love—God's love—let's see how human love and God's love differ.

HUMAN LOVE VS. GOD'S LOVE

Conditional vs. Unconditional

❣ Man's love is conditional.

"If you're a neat guy, I'll love you."
"If you're a cheerleader, I'll love you."
"Because you spend money on me, I'll love you."
"Because you act right, smell right, and look right, I'll love you."

♥ God's love is unconditional.

Read Romans 5:8. God's unconditional love means that He loves you no matter what. You don't deserve it. God loves you, warts and all.

Unconditional love doesn't have anything to do with how you see yourself, either. Whether you think you're the greatest thing that's happened since peanut butter or a "low-life piece of junk," God loves you.

Stingy vs. Sacrificial

💔 Man's love is stingy.

"If nothing else comes up, I may spend some time with you—even buy you a gift (if it doesn't cost too much). But I'm not making any promises." Stingy love holds back. You can't count on it when the going gets tough. It looks good only on the surface.

♥ God's love is sacrificial.

 Read John 3:16. Look at the Cross of Jesus. What a picture of sacrifice! God says, "I love you so much that I willingly gave My Son for you." God's Son was His greatest treasure... and He gave Him up for you!

Selfish vs. Serving

💔 Man's love is selfish.

Selfish love operates on the philosophy, "If you scratch my back, I'll scratch yours." Selfish love has ulterior motives. It says, "I want what I want when I want it." It gives only if something can be gained in return.

♥ God's love is serving.

 Read John 13:1. Serving love expects nothing in return, and often expresses itself through the most humbling tasks. Jesus demonstrated such servant love when He washed His disciples' feet (John 13:1-17).

That was a humbling act. He did it to show what serving love is.

God is always there when you need Him. He is never too busy to be interrupted. He is always willing to help you.

Grudging vs. Forgiving

💔 Man's love is grudging.

A person who has been betrayed by his best friend, or separated from a parent through divorce, can become bitter. If he/she continues to hold a grudge, he/she is really saying, "I'll never forgive him/her."

♥ God's love is forgiving.

Read Colossians 2:13-14. Some people think that some things they've done are so bad that God will never forgive them. But HE WILL. Remember His promise, "If we confess our sins, He is faithful and just and will forgive us our sins and purify us from all unrighteousness" (I John I:9). God's love is so great that He'll forgive us and remove all our guilt.

Limited vs. Creative

💔 Man's love is limited.

When a young person who can't get along with his parents says, "I'm going to love them if it's the last thing I do," it usually is. Just when he thinks he's got it all under control, he blows up at his mom, then sulks in his room. Trying to love without God's love is impossible.

💜 God's love is creative.

Read 2 Corinthians 5:16-17. When you allow God's love for you to soak in, it will flow through you and out to others. God's love can change your life so much that you'll have the capacity to love anyone (parents, ex-friends, enemies) in any situation—and not just a drop of love here and there, but a flood of it.

LOVE MADE TANGIBLE

You can think about love all you want, but that isn't enough. You've got to make it touchable, tangible. Jesus gave His followers the two greatest commandments.

Read Mark 12:28-31. What are the two greatest commandments?

_____

_____

_____

Now let's examine that first commandment more closely. (We'll check out the second commandment next week.) In your own words, explain Jesus' first commandment (12:30).

_____

_____

_____

_____

WE LOVE

"We love because He first loved us" (1 John 4:19).

God loves you and wants you to love Him in return.

Love is a two-way street. If a guy dates a girl and finally gets the courage to say, "I love you," and the girl answers, "Buzz off," they don't have much of a relationship. When you don't express your love to God, you are, in a sense, telling Him to "buzz off."

Loving God halfheartedly won't do. He wants you to love Him with all of your heart, soul, mind, and strength (Mark 12:30).

Think about

what it means to love God with all your heart, soul, mind, and strength. Remember: God is love. He started this whole love business. And He is the One who gives you the ability to love.

MAKING IT PERSONAL

How can you love Him with all your heart (emotions)?

_____

_____

_____

How can you love Him with all your soul (personality, attitudes, habits)?

_____

_____

_____

_____

How can you love Him with all your mind (mental capacities, thoughts)?

_____

_____

_____

_____

How can you love Him with all your strength (physical body)?

_____

_____

_____

How can you show your love for God? Check it out in John 14:21. In
your own words, what does it say?

_____

_____

_____

_____

 Memorize John 3:16.

S E S S I O N   4

Loving yourself and others

Is there someone you're having a hard time loving right now? Put that person's name here:

_____

In Session 3 you explored the first great commandment Jesus gave His disciples –to love God with all your heart, soul, mind, and strength (Mark 12:28-30). But Jesus didn't stop there.

Read Mark 12:31. In your own words, what was Jesus' second command?

_____

_____

Sometimes a person has a hard time loving others because he has never learned to love and accept himself.

Not loving yourself means that you don't accept God's evaluation that you are a lovable and worthwhile person. If you don't accept yourself, you're likely to look for the imperfections in others and reject them for the very things you don't like about yourself. But remember, God is the source of love; He can give you the ability to love yourself and others too. Let's take a look.

LOVING YOURSELF

Right now, some of you guys are reading this and getting mental pictures of yourselves in front of the bathroom mirror "flexing your pecs." Some girls are staring into that mirror admiring your good looks. And you're asking, "Is that what it means to love myself?"

No! Love appreciates a person for who he or she is, not for what he or she *looks like*. To love yourself means to ACCEPT YOURSELF. But most people don't. Why don't they?

-> Because of appearance. "I'm too tall, skinny, short, fat, weird looking."

-> Because of parents. "My parents fight, are divorced, reject me."

-> Because of lack of abilities. "I'm dumb. I have no talent. I not only can't play the guitar; I can hardly play the radio."

So what happens? You begin to think. . .

-> *Other people are sharper, smarter, and better than I am, so what they do must be OK.* You accept the values and attitudes of the people around you.

-> *I'm miserable because of what my parents did to me, so I'll show them.* You begin to rebel against their authority.

-> *God made a mess out of me, so why should I mess with Him?* You get mad at God.

No one loves me!
I'm a mess!
Why can't I do things right?
I've no talent.
I'm depressed.
What am I gonna do?

Write down some specific things about yourself that you don't like.

_____

_____

_____

In spite of all these things, you can love yourself! Here's how:

1 **Affirm Yourself**

List all the things you do like about yourself and thank God for them. Be honest.

_____

_____

_____

2 **Affirm That Jesus Is in Your Life**

Realize that as Jesus lives in you, you are not only OK, but everything He needs to change about you, He can and will. Now make a list of those things about you that God needs to change; then thank God for His ability to change you.

_____

_____

_____

_____

3 **Act on What God Is Doing in You**

Remember, you can "be transformed" (Romans 12:2). Take action to let Jesus change your life.

For example, if you need to lose weight, get on a plan to lose it. Then depend on God to supply the strength and power you need.

What actions do you believe God wants you to take to change?

_____

_____

_____

4 **Thank God Every Day for the Way He Made You**

Someone once said, "God don't make no junk." And it's true! You are of great value in God's eyes! As you become aware of God's love for you, and begin to accept yourself on the basis of what Jesus is doing in you, you will become more free to love others.

Thank God for at least three valuable things about yourself.

_____

_____

_____

LOVING OTHERS

Because God loves us, we can love one another.

Read 1 John 4:1-19. What does God's Word teach about loving others?

_____

_____

Think about the person whose name you wrote on page 37. Are you

willing to let God help you love that person? If so, take the following
steps.

1 **Admit That You Need God's Love for That Person and Ask God for It**

Believe it or not, needs and weaknesses are good for you. Why?
Because they drive you to God. Just as hunger leads you to food,
weaknesses take you to the only One who can meet them – Jesus Christ.
The fact that His "power is made perfect in [your] weakness" (2
Corinthians 12:9) is something you can count on.

2 **Believe That God Has Answered Your Prayer and Has Given You His Unconditional Love**

Look at 1 John 5:14-15 and explain the main truth.

_____

_____

_____

_____

Is it God's will that you love the person you're having trouble loving? Of
course it is! God has, in fact, commanded that you do it! So, on the
promise of His Word, you can believe that you have received your request
for love for your "difficult" person.

Now read and explain Mark 11:24.

_____

_____

_____

_____

_____

_____

Believe it before you see it or feel it. Believe it because God said it.

3 Step out and love by Faith

One evidence that you're a Christian is that you express love for other people, even people you don't like (John 13:34-35). As you allow God's love to work in and through you, you will begin to love others with His kind of love.

What are five

MAKING IT PERSONAL

characteristics of God's kind of love?
(If you have trouble remembering,
check pages 31-33 in Session 3.)
God's love is:

1. _____

2. _____

3. _____

4. _____

5. _____

Think again about the person whose name you wrote on page 37. What are three specific actions you can take this week to show God's love to that person?

1. _____

_____

2. _____

_____

3. _____

_____

Memorize I John 3:23

S E S S I O N   5

ALIVE IN YOU!

Experiencing Christ living in you

What frustrations do you have as you face . . .

-> your parents?

_____

_____

-> your friends?

_____

_____

-> your school?

_____

_____

➤ your dating life?

_____

_____

➤ your self?

_____

_____

Look back over the things you just listed. Have your frustrations been caused by your own wrong attitudes or actions?

_____

_____

Some of your frustrations are caused by circumstances beyond your control—circumstances that frustrate everyone. But it's a pretty safe guess that a few of your frustrations are the result of saying or doing something wrong. Even the Apostle Paul had that problem. He said, "For what I want to do I do not do, but what I hate I do" (Romans 7:15).

Paul knew the problem so well. Also he knew the solution.

Look up Colossians 1:27 to find that solution. Write it here.

_____

Now for a closer look...

LIVING A CHRIST-LIKE LIFE

The secret to living a Christ-like life is that Jesus Christ is alive in you.

Following Jesus is not you doing your best for God. It is allowing God to do His best in you!

Now go to page 90 and read "The Guest Who Took Over." As you read, summarize what each section says to you about Christ living in you. Write your summaries after each of the rooms listed here.

-> The Den

_____

_____

_____

-> The Dining Room

_____

_____

_____

-> The Living Room

_____

_____

_____

-> The Workshop

_____

_____

_____

-> The Game Room

_____

_____

_____

-> The Hall Closet

_____

_____

_____

 GIVING CHRIST CONTROL

Allowing Christ to live in you daily is possible but not automatic.

-> Before you invited Christ into your life, He lived outside your life. Your life was controlled by "I" (self) and therefore was out of balance. The result: FRUSTRATION.

-> Then you asked Jesus to come into your life. "I" (self) stepped down. Christ took control, so your life began to have the balance that Jesus brings. The result: FULFILLMENT.

-> Then you sinned by taking control of your life again. Though Jesus is still there, He is in a corner, not in control. So your life is out of balance again. The result: FRUSTRATION.

Now you want to let Christ control your life again. Is it possible? Can He be constantly in control? YES!

When you find that you're taking control of your life and taking control away from Christ, follow these steps.

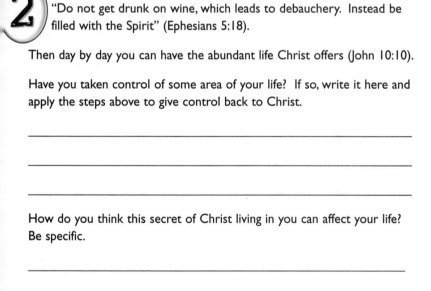

The secret to living a Christ-like life is that Jesus Christ is alive in you.

Confess Your Sin (Selfishness) to God

"If we confess our sins, He is faithful and just and will forgive us our sins and purify us from all unrighteousness" (1 John 1:9).

Release Control of Your Life to Christ

"Do not get drunk on wine, which leads to debauchery. Instead be filled with the Spirit" (Ephesians 5:18).

Then day by day you can have the abundant life Christ offers (John 10:10).

Have you taken control of some area of your life? If so, write it here and apply the steps above to give control back to Christ.

_____

_____

_____

How do you think this secret of Christ living in you can affect your life? Be specific.

_____

_____

_____

_____

CHRIST LIVING IN YOU

Read John 15:1-11

What is the key to Christ living in you? (15:4)

_____

_____

_____

What does it mean to "remain in"? (Some versions read "abide in".)
Check a Bible dictionary for a definition.

_____

_____

_____

What method does God use to develop Christ in your life? (15:2-3)

_____

_____

_____

What are the results of Christ living in you? (15:5-11)

_____

_____

_____

_____

_____

God

wants to cut some specific characteristics out of your life. They are called "the flesh" or "sinful nature." What are those characteristics? (See Galatians 5:19-21.) (Note: Check several Bible versions or a Bible dictionary to explain the characteristics you don't understand.)

MAKING IT PERSONAL

_____

_____

_____

_____

_____

_____

_____

_____

_____

_____

_____

_____

_____

_____

Which of those negative characteristics express themselves in your life? Be honest. Circle all that apply. Then ask God to rip them out of your life.

From Galatians 5:22-24, discover nine positive characteristics (fruit) that God wants to produce in your life.

_____

_____

_____

_____

_____

_____

_____

Which of these characteristics do you need most in your life? Rank them by renumbering from 1-9 according to your needs. (Let 1 represent your greatest need.)

How can these characteristics help you handle the frustrations you face with your parents, school, friends, etc.? Be specific.

_____

_____

_____

_____

_____

_____

_____

Now, based on this session, how can you cooperate with God to let the Holy Spirit develop what you discerned in these nine characteristics in your life? Be practical.

_____

_____

_____

_____

_____

_____

_____

Memorize John 15:5.

JESUS:

"I am the vine; you are the branches. If a man remains in me and I in him, he will bear much fruit; apart from me you can do nothing."

SESSION 6

Listening to God's Word

On Friday night, you are cruising with some friends from school. They stop and pick up a six-pack of beer. You want to be accepted by them, but don't want to drink. What would you do, and why?

_____

_____

_____

Jesus was tempted too. How did He handle it?

Read Matthew 4:1-10.

_____

_____

Read 1 Corinthians 10:13.

What can you do when you're tempted? Why?

_____

_____

Besides teaching you how to handle temptation, God's Word can help you in every situation you face in your life.

COUNTING ON GOD'S WORD

God's Word can help you because it is...

Inspired

1 INSPIRED means "God-breathed." God breathed the Bible into existence through His Spirit speaking to its writers. They wrote what God said to them.

> God's Word can help you in every situation you face in your life.

According to 2 Timothy 3:16-17, how can God's inspired Word help you?

_____

_____

_____

_____

_____

_____

Alive

2 Because God's Word is living and active, it can change your life in at least four areas. Look at Hebrews 4:12 to discuss what they are.

_____

_____

_____

_____

Authoritative

3 The Bible has authority because it comes from God. According to John 7:16-17 how can you personally find out if God's Word has authority?

_____

_____

_____

_____

True

4 God's Word is true. According to John 8:40, why is that?

_____

_____

Jesus tells us in John 8:31-32 what happens when you believe the truth of His Word. What does He say?

_____

_____

_____

_____

_____

> It's not the dusty Bible on the shelf but the Word of God in your heart that changes you.

DISCOVERING THE BENEFITS OF GOD'S WORD

 Following the example given, look up each Scripture listed on the chart below, and write down the benefits of getting to know God's Word and of applying God's Word to your life.

Benefits of The Word

Scripture	Benefits
Joshua 1:8	*I will be spiritually prosperous and successful.*
Psalm 1:1-3	
Psalm 119:1-2	
Psalm 119:63	
Psalm 119:97-105	
John 14:21	
John 15:3	
John 15:14	
Romans 10:17	
1 Peter 2:2	

EXPERIENCING THE BENEFITS OF GOD'S WORD

You can experience the benefits of God's Word by:
- ⇀⟩ Getting to know God's Word.
- ⇀⟩ Applying God's Word to your life.

Get to Know God's Word
You can know God's Word by taking these five actions:

 Hear. Listen carefully to reliable preachers and Bible teachers (Romans 10:17).

 Read. Get an overall view of the Bible by reading it consistently and underlining key passages (Acts 17:11).

 Study. Really dig into it. Ask the following questions:
- What does it say?
- What does it mean?
- How does it apply to me?
- What am I going to do in response?

 Memorize. Get started by mastering the verses assigned at the end of each session in this book. Learn each verse word perfect, and then review it every day for two months. For easy reference, cut out the memory cards provided in the back of this book.

 Meditate. As you meditate on God's Word, He will show you how it applies to you. God promises spiritual success and prosperity to everyone who meditates on Scripture (Joshua 1:8; Psalm 1:1-3). Here's how Scripture meditation works:

⇀⟩ Memorize the verse.

⇀⟩ Personalize the verse. Exchange the personal pronouns "you," "they," or "we" for the pronouns "I," "me," or your own name. **Example:** "How can a young man keep his way pure? By living according to Your

Word" (Psalm 119:9) becomes "How can I keep my way pure? By living according to Your Word."

Now look at Joshua 1:8 and personalize it below.

_____

_____

_____

➤ Visualize the verse. Draw it, or imagine yourself doing what it commands or having what it promises. Picture the situation in your mind.

➤ Actualize the verse. Ask God to make it real in your life. Bring it to mind often. Meditation stems from a word meaning "a cow chewing cud." So "chewing on it" will make it yours.

Apply God's Word

Read Luke 6:46-49 and James 1:22-25. Contrast the two kinds of people mentioned:

_____ vs. _____

Which kind of person would you rather be?

_____

_____

Think of some ways that you can become a "doer" of God's Word.

_____

_____

_____

_____

_____

_____

MAKING IT PERSONAL

To get God's Word into your life, begin reading and responding to a little bit of the Bible every day. Here's how to get started:

➡ Set aside just 10 minutes a day for the next 28 days to read and respond to the book of 1 John. (See page 96 for daily assignments.) Pick a specific time and place and record them below:

Time _____ Place _____

➡ Buy an inexpensive notebook. Each day, summarize your thoughts about those verses on one page in your notebook, using the Bible response sheet sample (page 98) as a guide.

➡ Set a goal of keeping your appointment with God and His Word for at least 10 days without missing.

 Memorize Psalm 119:9.

To Help You Communicate

A special notebook will help you in your communication with Jesus. You can order the *Time Alone with God Notebook* from Reach Out Youth Solutions.

• **www.reach-out.org**
• **1-800-473-9456**

S E S S I O N   7

Communicating through prayer

Who's your closest friend? Write his or her name below.

_____

What helped you develop the close relationship you have?

_____

_____

_____

_____

_____

_____

Developing a close relationship with God involves many of the same things – spending time together sharing:
    experiences
        thoughts
            feelings
                fears
                    joys.

Prayer is so important because it gives you an opportunity to talk with God, to get to know Him better, and to develop the ability to share everything with Him.

Relationships develop through communication. To know God, to become His friend and for Him to become your friend, means communicating with each other. How can you develop that communication? Answering these questions will help you communicate with God.

TO WHOM DO YOU PRAY?

God is your Friend; He wants to hear from you, and He listens to you. Yet He has power, wisdom, and understanding that no earthly friend can ever have (Revelation 5:12-13).

Because He is God, He has made some powerful promises to you. That's one way He speaks to you. Look up the following verses and paraphrase each of them so that they are personally meaningful to you.

John 14:13

_____

_____

_____

_____

John 15:7

_____

_____

_____

_____

John 16:24

_____

_____

_____

WHAT DO YOU PRAY FOR?

What are some things Jesus said you should pray for? Look at
Matthew 6:9-14.

_____

_____

_____

_____

_____

_____

_____

_____

Do you think it is possible for God not to answer your prayers? Why?

_____

_____

Compare your answer with John 15:7 and 1 John 5:14-15.

_____

_____

_____

WHEN DO YOU PRAY?

When do you think God wants to hear from you and speak to you?

_____

_____

David was a man "after [God's] own heart" (Acts 13:22). Look at the following verses to see when David prayed: Psalms 4:8; 5:3; 61:1-2; 69:13.

_____

_____

Was David always on top of life when he prayed? Look at Psalms 6:2; 8:1; 13:1; 18:3. What kinds of moods do you see?

_____

_____

_____

The bottom line is that God is always ready to hear from you and speak to you – wherever you are, however you're feeling, whenever you call on Him.

HOW DO YOU PRAY?

What clues does Jesus give us about how to pray in Mark 1:35?

_____

_____

_____

God desires for you to find out what He wants you to do. You do that by praying according to God's will. What do you think it means to pray "according to [God's] will"? (1 John 5:14)

_____

_____

_____

How do you know what God's choice, decision or purpose is? By praying.

Webster says. . . "according" means in harmony or agreement.

"Will" means choice, decision, or purpose.

So putting it together, praying "according to God's will" means to pray in harmony or agreement with God's choice, decision, or purpose.

Do you consider God your "best Friend" or "sort of an acquaintance"? Why?

_____

_____

_____

MAKING IT PERSONAL

_____

_____

_____

_____

How does that affect your prayer life?

_____

_____

_____

_____

_____

What three things did you learn in this session that will help you pray more effectively this week?

1. _____

_____

2. _____

_____

3. _____

_____

You can pray spontaneously—anytime, anywhere, under any circumstances. But also it's important to set aside a specific time each day to communicate with God through prayer. To get started, set aside just five minutes each day. Add this five-minute prayer time to the daily Bible reading time that you started last week.

Memorize John 16:24.

POWER TIP:

Begin each day meeting with God for prayer and Bible reading.

Becoming a disciple

What do you think about when you think of a "disciple?"

• A big, hairy fisherman?

• A little wimp with a black suit, black tie, and a sign on his back that says, "Tread on Me"?

• A person who stops doing 10 things she likes and starts doing 10 things she hates?

• A person who gives up everything and goes off to be a missionary in Africa?

• A wierdo who stands on the street and asks people if they're going to heaven or hell?

WHAT IS A DISCIPLE?

Deciding to invite Jesus Christ into your life is a very important step. But it's just the introduction. To develop a deep relationship with Jesus, you must learn how to get to know Him better. Following Jesus makes you a disciple.

Look up "disciple" in *Webster's* dictionary and in a Bible dictionary. Then read Matthew 4:19. From those three resources, define "disciple":

_____

_____

_____

_____

_____

Your definition should include these two ideas:

➛ A disciple is a learner and follower. So a disciple of Jesus spends time learning about Him and from Him and, as a result, willingly follows Him.

➛ A disciple teaches others. He passes on to other people what he learns from and about Jesus so they, in turn, can receive it and pass it on to others.

A DISCIPLE IS:

One maturing believer helping another believer mature so he, in turn, will be able to help others mature.

The Gospel of John gives some definite characteristics of a disciple. Look up each of the following passages in John. Record the characteristics, then write a phrase telling why you want that characteristic in your life.

Characteristics of A Disciple

Passage	Characteristic	Why I want it
2:11		
6:65-69		
8:31-32		
13:34-35		
14:15, 21		
15:1-8		
17:20-21		
20:19-22		
21:15-19		

Check This Out:

God is not so concerned about how far down the road you are, but that you're moving forward on the right road. If you follow Him down the road of discipleship, He will make a mature disciple of you.

HOW DO YOU MATURE AS A DISCIPLE?

Think about when you first received Jesus. What were you like in your new relationship to Him?

_____

_____

_____

Read Colossians 2:6. What attitude do you need now to mature as a disciple?

Your life will demonstrate SIMPLE FAITH and TOTAL TRUST in Christ.

Check Colossians 2:7 for the four elements necessary to "continue to live in Him." List them.

1. _____

2. _____

3. _____

4. _____

If you focus on these elements in your life, what trap will you not fall into? **Read Colossians 2:8.**

_____

_____

What are some philosophies, lies, and human traditions at school and among your friends that hinder you as a disciple?

_____

_____

Read Colossians 2:9-10.

What hope do you have of overcoming those hindrances?

_____

_____

HOT TIP:

Giving Jesus the freedom to express the fullness of His life in you is what develops you as a disciple.

WHAT IS THE COST OF MATURING AS A BELIEVER?

What are some fears you have about becoming a 100-percent-sold-out disciple of Jesus Christ?

_____

_____

_____

_____

In spite of any fears you may have, are you willing to become a 100-percent-sold-out disciple, letting Christ live fully in you? (Check one.)

_____ YES

_____NO

_____NOT SURE

If you couldn't answer YES, talk about your fears with a mature Christian you respect (your discipleship group leader). It's important that you work this out before going on with this book.

If you answered YES, press on.

Look at Luke 9:23-26 to grasp what it costs to be a 100-percent-sold-out disciple. Write what you discover.

_____

_____

_____

_____

Here are some thoughts from Luke 9:23-26 to go with your ideas:

Jesus said that if a person decides to follow Him, it will cost him:

-> his selfish pleasures —"deny himself"

-> ownership of his life —"take up his cross"

-> his goals and plans —"follow Me"

-> his reputation and status in life—"whoever loses his life for Me"

-> his time, talents, energy, money—all he has—"what does it profit a man to gain the whole world and lose his own soul?"

What do you need to give Jesus so you can follow Him completely?

_____

_____

_____

_____

WHAT RESULTS FROM BECOMING A MATURE DISCIPLE?

The cost of discipleship is not negative when you consider that by giving up your life, you actually save it. As you have discovered during the past few weeks, in exchange for your life, Jesus Christ gives you His life full of benefits that you can't find anywhere else. In exchange for your life, you receive the life of Jesus Christ.

Read Colossians 3:1-17. This gives a beautiful picture of what happens to you in the process of becoming a disciple.

➠ You become confident that your old life is dead and that your new life is hidden with Christ in God (Colossians 3:1-3). Explain these verses in your own words.

_____

_____

_____

➠ Christ is ridding your life of negative characteristics. What are they? (Colossians 3:5-11)

_____

_____

_____

_____

_____

➠ Christ is giving you new, positive characteristics as His disciple (3:12-16). List them.

_____

_____

_____

_____

_____

_____

_____

Christ living in you is what makes you a disciple.

⇢〉 What will make these new qualities a reality in your life? (3:17)

_____

_____

_____   _____

Ask
God to continue to give you the desire to be His 100-percent-sold-out follower. Pray for more of that desire.

Realize that it is the life of Jesus in you that makes you a disciple.

MAKING IT PERSONAL

Review this session, asking God to show you two qualities He wants to build into your life to make you a better disciple. Write them here.

1. _____

2. _____

Ask God to show you two ways that He wants to use you as a disciple to share His life with others. Write those ways.

1. _____

2. _____

Memorize Matthew 4:19.

"It takes six months to grow a squash. It takes a lifetime to grow an oak tree."
Miles Stanford

S E S S I O N 9

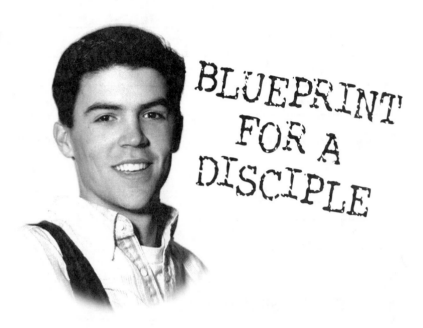

BLUEPRINT
FOR A
DISCIPLE

Knowing God's will for your life

Describe one tough decision you have had to make.

_____

_____

_____

How did you make it?

_____

_____

_____

_____

What happened as a result?

_____

_____

_____

_____

What, if anything, would you have done differently as you look back on it? Why?

_____

_____

_____

_____

YOU'RE IN GOD'S WILL IF . . .

As a follower of Jesus, you want to do what pleases God. And because He is your Father, He cares about the decisions you make and how you live your life.

God is also your Creator. He knows exactly why He created you. So it only makes sense that you can find real happiness and fulfillment by doing His will.

Romans 12:1-2 outlines how to know if you're in God's will. Read the passage, then answer the questions.

You're In God's Will If . . .

You Are Saved

"God's mercy" (Romans 12:1) means that Jesus died to save you from yourself and your sins.

According to John 6:40, what is God's will for you and how do you get in on it?

_____

_____

_____

You Are Sanctified

God wants you to "offer yourself…holy and pleasing" (Romans 12:1).

Define _sanctified_. Look it up in a Bible dictionary.

_____

_____

_____

According to 1 Thessalonians 4:3-8, what does "holy" mean concerning God's will for your life?

_____

_____

_____

You Will Suffer

Your body is a "living sacrifice" (Romans 12:1). This implies suffering—living under pressure.

Look at 1 Peter 2:20-21. What do those verses say about God's will for your life?

_____

_____

_____

You Are Spirit-filled

4

God wants you to be "transformed" (Romans 12:2). That means you are changed on the outside because of what the Holy Spirit is doing on the inside.

Look at Ephesians 5:17-18. What is God's will for you?

_____

_____

You Change Your Thinking

5

As you're saved, sanctified, suffering, and Spirit-filled you will "be transformed by the renewing of your mind." That's how you know God's will (Romans 12:2).

Look at Matthew 26:39-42. What quality do you see in Jesus' life that caused Him to do God's will even though it meant death?

_____

_____

_____

Look at James 4:7-8. What do you need to do to submit to God?

_____

_____

_____

_____

MAKING DECISIONS THAT PLEASE GOD

Now that you've looked at God's will for every Christian, how can you know His specific will for you?

You will make decisions about your future, marriage, college, work, friends, dates. Some decisions are big; some are small. But they are all important.

Clues in Proverbs 3:5-8 reveal how you can know what God wants you to do.

Trust God

"Trust in the Lord with all your heart" (Proverbs 3:5a).

Check out Psalms 86:15, 145:3, and Jeremiah 32:17.

Why can you trust God?

_____

_____

_____

_____

List All of the Options

"Lean not on your own understanding" (Proverbs 3:5b).

Read Proverbs 3:7.

What three steps do you need to take in order not to rely on your own understanding?

_____

_____

_____

3 Give the Options to God

"In all your ways acknowledge Him" (Proverbs 3:6a).

See Psalm 46:10. How can you do this?

_____

_____

_____

4 Wait for God's Solution

"He will make your paths straight" (Proverbs 3:6b).

What do the promises from God in the chart below mean to you?

God's Promises

Promise	Meaning to Me
Psalm 32:8	
Proverbs 5:21	
Isaiah 30:21	
Jeremiah 29:11	

Enjoy Confidence in the Decision

"This will bring health to your body and nourishment to your bones" (Proverbs 3:8).

Look at 1 Corinthians 14:33. What does your decision mean if there is confusion?

_____

_____

_____

_____

_____

Look at Colossians 3:15. What will be the result of a correct decision?

_____

_____

Look at James 1:5-8. If you have followed these steps, of what can you be confident?

_____

_____

_____

Big doors open on small hinges.

What is one

difficult decision you are making
right now? Explain it here:

MAKING IT PERSONAL

_____

_____

_____

Using the clues from Proverbs 3:5-8, work through your decision. Be
specific.

1. Trust God. How are you going to trust God in this decision?

_____

_____

_____

2. List all of the options. Write the options below.

_____

_____

_____

_____

_____

_____

3. Give the options to God. Describe what you intend to do to turn it over to God.

_____

_____

_____

4. Wait for God's solution. What Bible promise has God given you about this situation?

_____

_____

_____

5. Enjoy confidence in the decision. Describe the confidence you have in this decision now that you have followed God's will. (If you don't have confidence in the decision, go back to Proverbs 3:5-8 and begin again.)

_____

_____

_____

God may not answer immediately. He may want you to wait for His timing.

Tips To Find God's Will

1. Prayer, the Bible, advice from others, and circumstances will help you make your decisions.

2. God doesn't hide His will from you.

3. You don't have to be afraid of His will, because it brings joy.

4. God's will is not a map that you will suddenly discover one day. It's a step-by-step process.

5. Don't throw away your brain to learn God's will, but let your mind be Spirit-controlled.

6. Even when you are in God's will, you can't expect all your problems will magically go away.

7. If none of the options is God's will, don't panic—wait on the Lord.

 Memorize Proverbs 3:5-6.

SESSION 10

GOOD, BETTER, BEST

Setting goals and priorities

How do you think most students in your school define "success"?

_____

_____

_____

_____

Do you agree with that definition? How does your own definition differ?

_____

_____

_____

_____

_____

Do you feel that your definition of success is accurate? Why?

_____

_____

_____

_____

How do you know when you have achieved success?

_____

_____

_____

_____

God sees you as very important. He made a great sacrifice on the cross to establish a relationship with you. Because of His sacrifice and love, His view of success for you is more important than anyone else's view.

DEVELOPING A LIFE GOAL

Success means you have a goal to achieve.

What are some goals you've set for yourself?

_____

_____

_____

_____

_____

God has some goals for you as one of His children. Let's take a look at those goals from His point of view. Find one of God's goals for you in each of the following verses.

➥ Matthew 6:33 _____

_____

➥ Romans 8:29 _____

_____

➥ I Corinthians 10:31 _____

_____

➥ Philippians 3:10 _____

_____

What common goal runs through all of these verses?

_____

_____

Using the verses and goals just listed, write a life goal for yourself. Word it so it will fit on a t-shirt.

MY LIFE GOAL

_____

_____

_____

Think about that goal for a minute. If you set out to meet that goal, what are the first three steps you would take?

1. _____

_____

2. _____

_____

3. _____

_____

How could your life change if you took such steps?

_____

_____

_____

_____

SETTING PRIORITIES

"Jesus grew in wisdom and stature, and in favor with God and man" (Luke 2:52). That means Jesus was growing
        intellectually
          physically
            spiritually
              socially.

On the following Activities List, write the main things you do in each of these four areas. (For example, under "Intellectually," you might write: "Make good grades at school; spend 20 hours a week watching TV; read the comics and sports pages of the newspaper.")

Put each activity on your Activities List in priority. Number them according to their order of importance and value to you. Make a note beside each activity expressing how it relates to your life goal. Circle any item on your Priorities List that conflicts with that goal.

ACTIVITIES LIST

Area	Activity	Priority	Life Goal Relationship
Intellectually			
• _____	_____	_____	
• _____	_____	_____	
• _____	_____	_____	
Physically			
• _____	_____	_____	
• _____	_____	_____	
• _____	_____	_____	
Spiritually			
• _____	_____	_____	
• _____	_____	_____	
• _____	_____	_____	
Socially			
• _____	_____	_____	
• _____	_____	_____	
• _____	_____	_____	
_____	_____	_____	
Other Activities			
• _____	_____	_____	
• _____	_____	_____	
• _____	_____	_____	

Rewrite

MAKING IT PERSONAL

your priorities in light of pursuing Jesus as your life goal. Write them below. (NOTE: Delete things from your original list that will not be helpful in accomplishing your goal. You may need to add some things you're not doing that you believe God wants you to do.)

Now, pray through that list, giving each priority to the Lord. Give Him the freedom to change your priorities as you grow in Him.

JESUS–FIRST PRIORITIES LIST

1. _____
2. _____
3. _____
4. _____
5. _____
6. _____
7. _____
8. _____
9. _____
10. _____
11. _____
12. _____

If one of your priorities is to know God better, one way to do that is to spend time with Him.

Make a commitment to continue spending 15 minutes a day with the Lord.

☐ Check here if you intend to spend 15 minutes with God daily.

Student's Time Alone With God

The next book in this series, *Spending Time Alone with God,* will help make the time you spend with God more and more meaningful. Go for it! Order it from www.reach-out.org or call 1-800-473-9456.

Memorize Matthew 6:33.

THE GUEST WHO TOOK OVER
What happened when Jesus came to live in me

By Steve Lawhead

Saturday, December 6

Today, I made up my mind. I'm going to invite Jesus into my life. Now, I've got a big, rambling ranch-style life with a lot of rooms. I'm sure I can make Him feel at home. I've put new curtains in the guest room and everything's ready. He'll like living with me.

Sunday, December 7

He arrived just like He said He would; He came right in—added a little class to my life. I'm sure glad I asked Him. There may be a few little things to rearrange, but I'm sure we'll get along just fine.

Wednesday, December 10

It has come to my attention that He doesn't want to stay in His room all the time. I didn't know what to do. He'd be comfortable there, but He said, "I didn't come here to be a guest. If I'm going to live here, I'd like to see the rest of the house." I reacted at first but, after thinking it over, I wouldn't want to stay cooped up in the guest room either.

Thursday, December 11

Last night I took Him to the DEN. It's one of my favorite rooms, so I thought for sure He'd like it. It's a cozy room, not large at all, with deep leather chairs—good for reading and thinking.

He came in with me and started looking around. He went over to the bookshelf and picked up one of my magazines. That made me a little nervous, to say the least. Then He went over and looked at the pictures on the wall. He cast a doubtful eye at my gun-and-knife collection, and that did it. He didn't say anything, but I felt pressure to please such an important guest. I blurted out, "You know, Jesus, I've been meaning to do a little redecorating in here. Perhaps You would like to have a say in it too?" He replied, "I'd be delighted to help you out. But I'm afraid some of these things will have to go."

"Just say the word and they're gone," I told Him. What a relief.

Tuesday, December 16

I'd been planning to have Him down for a banquet in the DINING ROOM as soon as He settled in. Last night was the night. It was fantastic! I had really outdone myself—that's what I figured. The Lord didn't seem to enjoy it as much as I'd hoped He would. Not at first, anyway.

Before dinner, we had some appetizers. Nothing fancy, --just some potato chips and onion dip, some cheese crunchies, pretzels, and taco fluffies. We were munching away when He asked me, "What are we having for dinner?"

I told Him, "We're having pizza and french fries, a whole can of pork and beans, and for dessert—chocolate-covered doughnuts with raspberry ice cream and marshmallow sauce. Later on we'll have some popcorn and cotton candy for a snack." I had no sooner read off the menu than I saw Him frowning. "Did I leave anything out, Jesus?" I asked Him.

"No, not a thing." He laughed. "I couldn't help noticing that everything you were planning on serving was insubstantial junk. Garbage, as food. Where's the meat? Vegetables? Bread? That's what you really need."

"B-but," I stuttered, "I like this food. I eat it all the time."

"Look," Jesus said, getting up, "show Me where the kitchen is and I'll fix you something that will put meat on your bones. You've been indulging your shallow appetites and desires too long. I think you'll find the change rewarding."

He went in and made the most delicious meal, using the meat and vegetables of God's will and the bread of the Scripture. I must admit it was satisfying. I plan to be eating better now that He is here.

Wednesday, December 17

Tonight after supper I took the Lord into the LIVING ROOM. He liked it at once—called it the fellowship room. He said, "We'll talk and pray and really get to know each other well."

I thought it was a terrific idea at the time, so I told Him, "That suits me just fine, Lord." And we sat down and had the best talk I can remember having.

Tuesday, December 23

Tonight I was heading to the first of two parties. As I came down the hall, I happened to glance through the door of the living room and saw Jesus sitting on the couch. He wasn't reading or anything, just sitting there waiting. I poked my head in the door. "Waiting for someone?"

"Yes, as a matter of fact, I was waiting for you," He said.

"Me?" I asked. I hadn't the faintest idea what He was talking about. "I'm going out to a party," I told Him. Then it hit me. Since our first time together, I had neglected our fellowship time together. He had waited for me every evening while I went on my way. My face turned crimson with embarrassment.

"I'm dreadfully sorry," I said. "Please forgive me for keeping You waiting."

"I forgive you," He said. "Now sit with Me, if only a few moments, and we'll pray before you have to leave."

Monday, December 29

Had the day off today, so I thought I'd spend a few hours puttering around the WORKSHOP. Jesus met me at the basement door, just as I was starting down. I figured that, being a carpenter by trade, He'd like to see my tools. Indeed, He was impressed with how well-stocked my workshop was.

"I am very proud of my workshop," I told Him. "I've got the tools and materials you need to do almost anything."

"Wonderful!" Jesus said. He glanced around the basement room and, looking rather disappointed, declared, "I don't see anything you've made."

"Well, I made these." I brought out three balsa wood airplanes.

"Is that all? I expected a person as well-equipped as you to have done much more than that," He said sadly.

"I like toys, so I make them," I told Him frankly. "I don't know how to make anything else. A lot of tools are useless for me, I'm afraid. I've never had the skills to use them."

His face broke into a smile. "You'll learn," He said encouragingly, "because I'll teach you. You must do what I do." I've got to say, He does know His business. I'm often amazed at how well things turn out when He is guiding me through the steps. I'm going to learn a lot, I can tell.

Wednesday, December 31

Big party tonight! We're going to bring the new year in right! All my friends will be there and we'll get it on.

Thursday, January 1

I feel terrible. Last night wasn't a good night and I didn't have any fun. What happened was this:

I was throwing this shindig in my GAME ROOM and most of the guests had arrived. Gossip was making out with Lust on the couch. Arrogance and Envy were playing Ping-Pong and yelling at each other. Drunkenness was standing on top of the TV singing, "I Can't Get No Satisfaction," at the top of his lungs. Depravity, with his obscene jokes and weird sense of humor, was on the way.

Things were just getting wound up for the evening when in walked Christ. I had forgotten all about Him. I guess I knew what kind of party it would be, so I just didn't invite Him. He looked around with an expression on His face like "I've seen it all before." He came over and asked me, "You enjoy this kind of thing?"

"Well, it's OK for laughs," I said. My friends were listening and I didn't want to hurt their feelings. "Nothing serious. It's just for fun."

"Is it?" He asked.

"Is it what?" I didn't know what He was talking about.

"Is it fun?" He looked at me hard and I just couldn't lie.

"Well, not really," I told Him. "I used to think so, but not anymore."

"You want to have fun? I invented fun," He told me. "I'll introduce you to some of My friends. We'll show you what fun is meant to be."

I'm ashamed at what I did next. I turned Him off. I just walked away and left Him standing there. I ignored Him and, after a while, He left. I don't know now why I did it. It just seemed as if He were asking too much. To tell the truth, at the time I was having second thoughts about the arrangement.

But my evening was ruined. I didn't enjoy myself at all. I didn't sleep well last night either. So I got up early and patched things up with Jesus, and while I don't feel much better about it, He assures me He'll help me get over it.

Wednesday, January 7

I was on my way to meet Jesus in the living room this morning when He stopped me in the hall. There was a pained expression on His face, and I could see that something was troubling Him.

"What's the matter?"

"There's something dead around here," He said. "I can smell it. A rat or something has crawled in and died in your HALL closet."

Panic set in. I knew what was in my closet and I didn't want Him to look in there. "Oh, it's probably nothing, Lord," I assured Him. "Let's go into the living room and talk."

"I want to talk about what's in your closet," He said. He was firm.

"Well, it's really nothing, uh—just some antiques."

"Antiques?" He said the word and looked right through me, reading my thoughts.

"Yeah, just a few personal things," I said, trying to keep up the deception. "After all, it's none of Your business." That was the wrong thing to say for sure. I knew that as soon as I had said it.

He disregarded the comment completely. "You don't expect Me to live here with something dead in the closet, do you?" Then He smiled. "I think your 'antiques' are a little moldy and it's time to get rid of them. Let's clean the closet."

"Oh, Lord, I know I should throw them out, but I just can't. I haven't got the strength. Can't You handle it? I'm afraid. I hate to ask, but. . . ."

"Say no more. Just give Me the key and I'll do the rest. I don't mind a bit."

He did it all. Cleaned out the hall closet and never once mentioned a word about it. Lately I've been thinking of giving Him the deed to this place—giving it all to Him. I'm sure He could run it better than I do. What do you think He would say if I asked Him?

Adapted from *My Heart—Christ's Home* by Robert Boyd Munger.
© 1954 by Inter-Varsity Christian Fellowship of the U.S.A. and used by permission of InterVarsity Press.

1 JOHN

DAILY BIBLE READINGS

(For use with the Bible Response Sheet)

DAY	BIBLE PASSAGE	DAY	BIBLE PASSAGE
1	1:1-4	15	3:15-18
2	1:5-10	16	3:19-24
3	2:1-6	17	4:1-3
4	2:7-11	18	4:4-6
5	2:12-14	19	4:7-12
6	2:15-17	20	4:13-16
7	2:18-20	21	4:17-21
8	2:21-25	22	5:1-3
9	2:26-27	23	5:4-5
10	2:28-29	24	5:6-8
11	3:1-3	25	5:9-12
12	3:4-8	26	5:13-15
13	3:9-10	27	5:16-17
14	3:11-14	28	5:18-21

BIBLE MEMORY CARDS

Each memory verse on these cards is printed in the *New International Version* (NIV). The verses correspond with the Bible studies in this book.

ALWAYS CARRY THE CARDS WITH YOU.

Use what helps you most:

- ➤ Put a rubber band around them.

- ➤ Carry them in an envelope.

- ➤ Place them in your wallet or pocket book.

- ➤ Put them on the visor of your car.

- ➤ Carry them in your Bible.

- ➤ Daily review each verse you've learned.

- ➤ Have someone check your progress each week.

- ➤ Apply each verse to your daily life.

BIBLE RESPONSE SHEET

Date _____

Passage _____

Title _____

Key Verse _____

Summary _____

_____

_____

_____

_____

_____

_____

_____

_____

_____

Personal Application _____

_____

_____

_____

_____

_____

_____

_____

_____

_____

_____

1. SALVATION
1 John 5:11

And this is the testimony: God has given us eternal life, and this life is in His Son. (NIV)

2. GOD'S PURPOSES
Philippians 1:6

Being confident of this, that He who began a good work in you will carry it on to completion until the day of Christ Jesus. (NIV)

3. GOD'S LOVE
John 3:16

For God so loved the world that He gave His one and only Son, that who-ever believes in Him shall not perish but have eternal life. (NIV)

4. LOVING OTHERS
1 John 3:23

And this is His command: to believe in the name of His Son, Jesus Christ, and to love one another as He commanded us. (NIV)

5. CHRIST IN YOU
John 15:5

I am the vine; you are the branches. If a man remains in Me and I in him, he will bear much fruit; apart from Me you can do nothing. (NIV)

6. GOD'S WORD
Psalm 119:9

How can a young man keep his way pure? By living according to your Word. (NIV)

7. PRAYER
John 16:24

Until now you have not asked for anything in My name. Ask and you will receive, and your joy will be complete. (NIV)

8. DISCIPLESHIP
Matthew 4:19

"Come, follow Me," Jesus said, "and I will make you fishers of men." (NIV)

9. GOD'S WILL
Proverbs 3:5-6

Trust in the Lord with all your heart and lean not on your own under-standing; in all your ways acknowledge Him, and He will make your paths straight. (NIV)

10. PRIORITIES
Matthew 6:33

But seek first His kingdom and His righteousness, and all these things will be given to you as well. (NIV)

What's Next?

Congratulations for completing *Following Jesus*. Your adventure in Moving Toward Maturity continues with *Spending Time Alone With God*.

How can you deepen your relationship with Jesus? Time! Just like all other relationships, you get to know Jesus intimately when you spend time with Him. Jesus wants to draw near to you as you draw near to Him! *Spending Time Alone with God* will help you spend time alone with God every day as you:

- ➔ Study the Bible
- ➔ Enjoy prayer
- ➔ Give thanks
- ➔ Pray for yourself
- ➔ Memorize Scripture
- ➔ Celebrate praise
- ➔ Confess your sins
- ➔ Pray for other people

To give you a practical tool for spending time alone with God you will need the *Time Alone with God Notebook*. This notebook will help you record your adventure with God.

See your youth leader to get both of these books or
order online at www.reach-out.org or by phone: 1-800-473-9456

The Complete Moving Toward Maturity Series

A six book progressive discipleship series that will move students to spiritual maturity in Christ

GETTING STARTED helps new believers successfully begin their walk with Christ.

FOLLOWING JESUS builds a solid foundation for a life-changing relationship with Christ and for becoming a disciple of Christ.

SPENDING TIME ALONE WITH GOD deepens students' relationship with Jesus by learning how to spend time with Him.

MAKING JESUS LORD challenges students to obey Jesus and give Him control in the day-to-day issues they face.

GIVING AWAY YOUR FAITH guides students on the wild adventure of overcoming their fears and taking the risk to boldly communicate Christ.

INFLUENCING YOUR WORLD shows students that they can become influential leaders through serving the needs of the people around them.

TIME ALONE WITH GOD NOTEBOOK gives students practical tools for guiding them in their adventure with God.

LEADER'S GUIDE gives the group leader all the reasons needed to lead a lively and life-changing discipleship group. This book contains the leader's material from all five books of the Moving Toward Maturity series

MOVING TOWARD MATURITY REFERENCE KIT contains all of the Moving Toward Maturity books plus six tapes designed to inspire you as a discipler of students.

For these and other books and resources:
Order online at **www.reach-out.org**
or by phone: 1-800-473-9456

Moving Toward Maturity Leader's Resources

LEADER'S GUIDE

What do I need to disciple students? Passion for God, love for kids, and this Leader's Guide! All of the resources you need to relate to your students, prepare for your group, and lead interactive, lively and life-changing discussions are in your hand. This book contains the leader's material for the five books in the Moving Toward Maturity series.

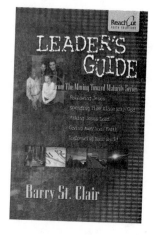

AUDIO KIT

The Audio Kit offers discipleship group leaders motivation for discipling students. Speakers Louie Giglio, Dave Busby and Barry St. Clair do not offer step-by-step instruction, instead, they prepare and inspire discipleship leaders at the heart level.

LEADER'S RESOURCE KIT

The Moving Toward Maturity Resource Kit contains all of the Moving Toward Maturity books plus six tapes designed to inspire you as a discipler of students.

For these and other books and resources:
Order online at **www.reach-out.org**
or by phone: **1-800-473-9456**

Life Happens— Get Ready

Do you think deciding what to do on Saturday is a long-range plan? That's normal. But the "biggies" will be decided in the next five years: college, job, lifelong friends, marriage partner (really scary!) That's why you need to answer these huge questions now: who am I? where am I going? how am I going to get there? *Life Happens* provides you with nine practical "destiny deciders" to help you discover God's unique destiny for your life. Spend a few minutes a day reading and writing in *LIfe Happens* and you'll start to see the fantastic life God has in store for you.

Taking Your Campus For Christ

Now that's a radical idea! It can happen. But it will take some radical people with radical love. Radical love. That's what your friends need. In this book you will find out how to have it and how to give it away. God wants to tap you on the shoulder, get you to look Him in the face, and challenge you to radically love your friends through the power of the Gospel.

You can make the difference at your school! Take the challenge to take your campus for Christ.

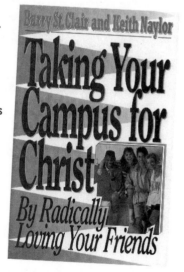

For these and other books and resources:
Order online at www.reach-out.org or by phone: 1-800-473-9456